You Would if You Loved Me

You Would if You Loved Me

Collected by Sol Gordon, Ph.D.

BANTAM BOOKS · LONDON · TORONTO · NEW YORK

RL 4, IL 8+

YOU WOULD IF YOU LOVED ME

A Bantam Book | September 1978
2nd printing .... August 1978
3rd printing . December 1978
4th printing ...... May 1980

ISBN 0-553-14186-4

Published simultaneously in the United States and Canada

Bantam Books are published by Bantam Books, Inc. Its trade-
mark, consisting of the words "Bantam Books" and the por-
trayal of a bantam, is Registered in U.S. Patent and Trademark
Office and in other countries. Marca Registrada. Bantam
Books, Inc., 666 Fifth Avenue, New York, New York 10019.

PRINTED IN THE UNITED STATES OF AMERICA

13 12 11 10 9 8 7 6 5 4

Introduction

In the so-called "good old days," the classic line was: "Want to see my etchings?" Strange, in a way—in those days no one had etchings and everyone knew it was a line. Nowadays, lots of people have etchings and this line is rarely used.

These days, lots of females fall for lines used on them. Of the many thousands I've collected, by far the most widely employed is: "If you really love me . . ."

Why am I so hot and bothered about this—and where do I get this stuff about females falling for lines? Sounds sexist, doesn't it? Well, maybe. But every year some 1,000,000 adolescent girls (under nineteen) become pregnant, with about 600,000 females giving birth, a statistic which says nothing about the one in four pregnancies among adults that are unintended. Among teenagers, pregnancies and births are almost always undesirable and unhealthy. Furthermore, of the some 3,000,000 new cases of VD each year, about two-thirds are among young people under twenty-five years of age.

My point? Females, not males, become pregnant. And it's the female who suffers the most. It is also true that almost all males abandon the teenagers they impregnate. Their line: "How do I know it was me?" Of course, males suffer too (mainly from treating females badly), and this may range from sexual dysfunction to the ultimate boredom—being stuck for a lifetime with an unliberated female.

Some females also use lines to seduce males, but this phenomenon is nothing compared with the forces that have built and maintained our double standard:

> Young males are "supposed" to have sex.
> Females are not.

> Males are "supposed" to seduce.
> Females are not supposed to even want to have sex.

Therefore, when girls are "overwhelmed," they are not prepared. Less than 20 percent of sexually active females regularly use effective contraception during their early sexual experiences. Yet, some people say it's the pill that makes girls "promiscuous." If only they would practice birth control, then we wouldn't be in so much trouble.

I began collecting lines ten years ago at a summer program for disadvantaged youth. We simply "advertised" the current lines used by the boys. By making them public, we had a lot of complaints from the boys that we were ruining their sex lives. But that summer our project had no pregnancies—perhaps the only such record among several hundred programs in the country.

Recently I suggested to Ann Landers that she collect lines from her readers. She received 18,000 letters! One woman criticized Ann Landers for printing a "how to" list for beginners. "Young boys are plenty aggressive these days," she wrote. "It's foolish to supply them with alternate 'lines' should theirs fail." Ann Landers' reply was, "The purpose of printing 'lines' was to wise up the naive and vulnerable who, too often, are snowed by cool cats on the make. Hopefully, if the girls see it in print, they will recognize it for what it is—just a line. And a fairly standard one at that."

I am encouraging females to think of their own lines. Not that I want this kind of interaction to remain a game, but rather to provide a transition—a "pause that refreshes," if you like—in order to give girls time to catch up and be able to say that it's all right for both men and women to want sex. But if sex is an option the following questions must be considered by both partners:

1. Are we ready?
2. Do we practice birth control?
3. Can we handle the consequences?
4. Do we want to have sex with anyone?
5. Are we in love? Does it matter?
6. Is it normal?
7. Should we wait?

If someone says, "If you really love me, you would . . . ," could your response be "If you really love me, you won't put pressure on me"?

Could it be that the next time a male says that he won't use a condom because he gets no feelings out of it, a female might respond, "What's the matter with you? All the other guys I know get plenty of feelings out of it."

Humor is, after all, the best way to relieve anxiety. If you are not anxious, you'll have time to cool off. And time, too, for birth or self control.

Enjoy.

Sol Gordon, Ph.D.
Professor of Child
and Family Studies
Syracuse University
June 1978

Rules for Lines

How Can You Tell If It's a Line?

If the *only way* you can prove your love is having sex, it's a line.

Threatened with rejection if you don't. . .? Then, the one who threatens is not in love with you and will most likely leave you after "it" anyway.

If you feel that it can't happen to you, it probably will.

"No" is still the best oral contraception. If you can't say no, say "yes" to birth control and condoms.

THE LINES

The Ditch Line

The line used by males who find their dates unattractive and want only one thing before they ditch them. When the lights are out, they say: "You have such beautiful eyes."

(Nice) Try Lines

With Female Replies

He (stroking female's arm languidly): These are only whispers, I know how to shout at you.
She: So shut-up already!

Him: I'd like to know you better—mind, body and soul.
Her: Oh, yeah? Then I suggest you take Psychology 205, Biology 123, and Religion 101.

He (at a drive-in movie): Would you like to get in the back seat?
She: No, I'd rather sit up here with you.

Fast Lines

Without Replies
(but with space available
for your response)

❧

Baby, you really mean a lot to me. I really care for you. I really love you.

Try it, you'll like it.

Why don't we get comfortable?

What's the matter, baby, are you scared?

Let's make tonight something to remember.

Honey, would you like to hold my drink for me while I light my cigarette?

Just because someone lives with a person doesn't mean they can't sleep with someone else.

Let's go to my place or your place.

Cold Lines

It's too cold out tonight; why don't I just sleep here?

You mean you're still a virgin? What are you, frigid?

Him: Are you cold?
Her: Yes.
Him: Well, let me warm you up.

Male: Gee, the apartment's cold tonight!
Female: Well, mine isn't.

Him: It's a long, cold walk back to my room.
Her: Want some mittens?

Male: Are you going to come over tonight? It's supposed to be so cold out.
Female: No, but I can give you a few extra blankets and my teddy bear.

He: The heat in my apartment has been turned off, and the bed's cold. How about warming it up?
She: Buy a heating pad. You turn me off.

Hot Lines

Male: Is it getting hot in here? Let's go for a walk.
Female: No, it's not hot in here. The heat is in your pants.

Firing Lines

Him: Want to go to the beach and watch the shooting stars?
Her: Sure—as long as it's only the stars that are doing the shooting.

(Good-) Bye Lines

Him: Just take it as an experience for the night. Everything will be the same between us tomorrow.
Her: If it's going to be the same tomorrow, why not let it be the same now?

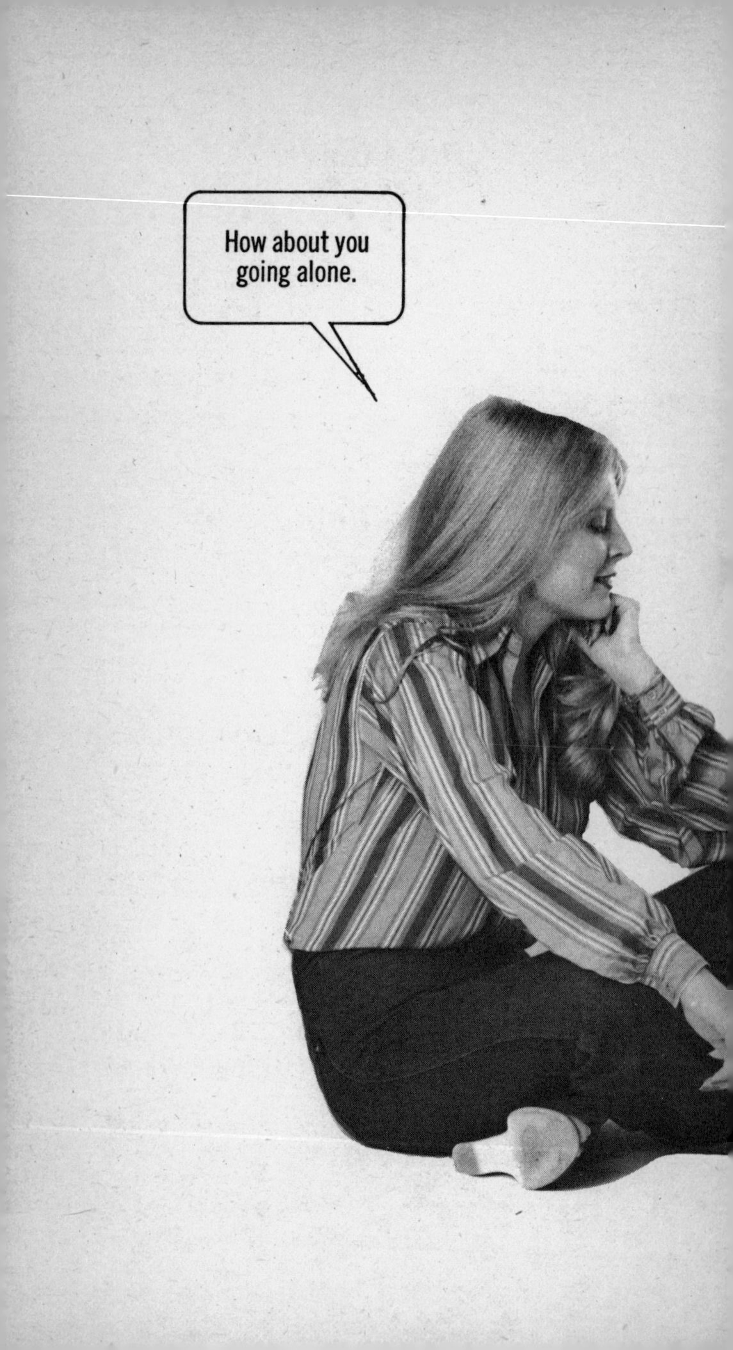
How about you going alone.

Male: Why don't you stay? I'll get you up for church.
Female: All right, Father.

He: Oh, you've got some sand on your mouth. Let me get it off for you.
She: Leave it there so nobody slips!

He: Wanna go to bed?
She: No, thanks. I just got up.

Him: Let's go back to my place and learn about each other.
Her: No thanks. I've learned all I need to know about you!

Male: How about a good-night screw.
Female: Good night, screw!

Front Lines

Male: If I told you you had a great body, would you hold it against me?
Female: Not at all. I usually find that first impressions are deceiving.

Back Lines

Him: I would like to get into your pants.
Her: No, thanks. One rear end is enough!

Side Lines

He: Hey, I'm a geology major. You wanna come over and see my rocks?
She: No, thanks. I'd rather stay at home and get stoned!

Male: Why don't we go down to the docks and watch the submarine races?
Female: Sorry, tonight's match was canceled due to lack of an opponent.

Work Lines

Let's go see if you've cleaned up your room.

He: How'd you like to come over for dinner?
She: Sure, as long as we only eat dinner.

Him: How about coming over and bringing your toothbrush?
Her: Why? Do you want me to scrub the floor with it?

<u>Play Lines</u>

❧❦❧

He: Wanna have some fun tonight?
She: Let's make popcorn!

Let's tickle. You've never been tickled like this before.

He: Hey, baby, wanna pretend my bed's a tree and kiss in between the limbs?
She: Sorry, squirrel, I'm not a nut.

Male: Do you play games?
Female: Let's play house and you're home alone.

If you show me yours, I'll show you mine.

You're a tease. So let's see what it is and if it's all that good!

Him: Hey, baby, how about a little in-and-out play?
Her: Sure, creep, just keep moving out the door while I go in my apartment.

He: Want to watch the corn grow and see if we can't get the kernels popping?
She: A corny invitation should be saved for squirrels.

Sport Lines

Sex is invigorating. It's just like any other kind of exercise—we should practice.

I really give a great back-rub—but you have to undo your bra.

Why are you saving it? The more you exercise it, the longer it stays in shape.

Male: Wanna go upstairs and check out my new water bed?
Female: Nope—I don't swim.

Male: Oh, come on; it's good exercise!
Female: No, thanks. I played tennis this afternoon.

Him: What could be more natural than going for a swim?
Her: Why? You're all wet already.

Male: I just oiled my machine. Want to see how it works?
Female: Why don't you give it a cold shower and see if it rusts?

He: Would a cute thing like you happen to know where I could cut some grass?
She: My front lawn, tomorrow morning.

15

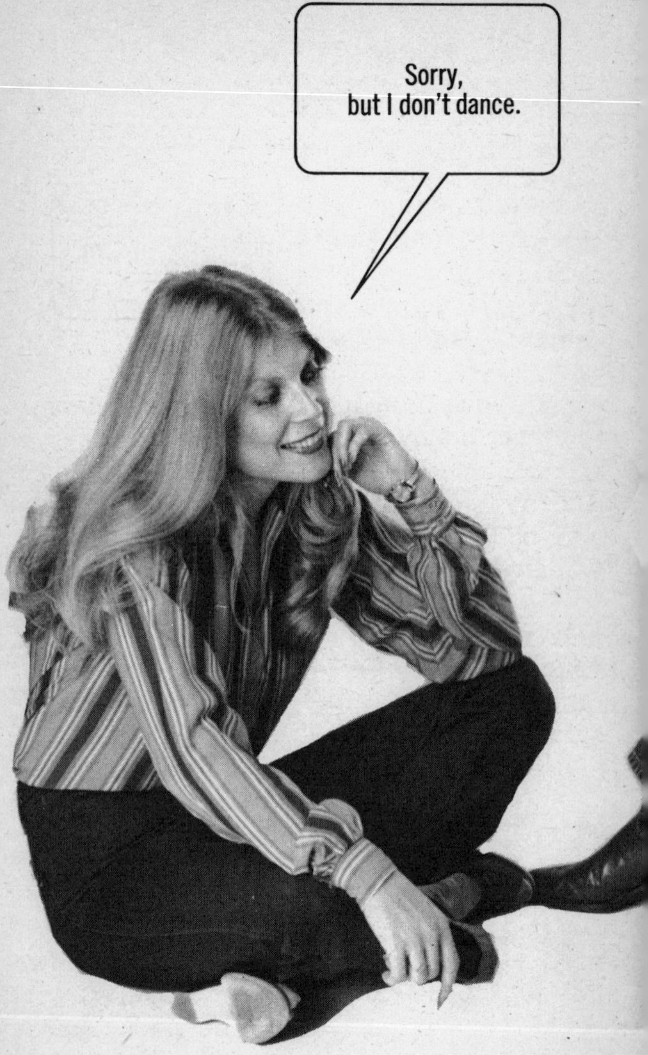
Sorry,
but I don't dance.

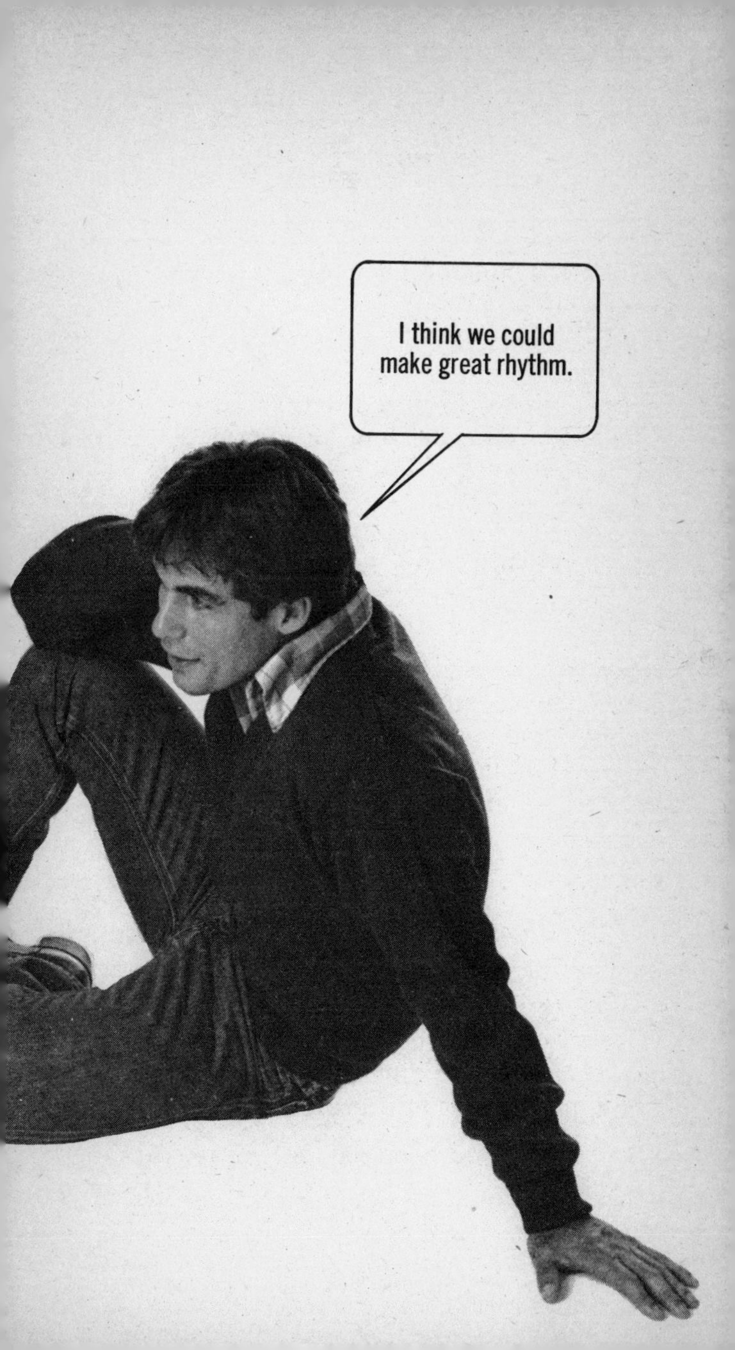
I think we could make great rhythm.

Medical Lines

Him: It's late and I'd really like to get to know you better.
Her: Not tonight. I have a headache.

I have a card from the Red Cross that says I'm negative. It means I have no sperm. So I can't get you pregnant.

Look, baby, I am having these real bad headaches. If you make love to me, my headache would stop.

Him: How would you like to play doctor?
Her: I'm not sick.

Female: Why don't you use a rubber?
Male: I'm allergic to them.

Health Lines

Sex builds up your muscles.

Sex makes your hair grow.

Sex makes you have a good complexion.

Sex burns up a lot of calories.

Religious Lines

The same God who put these desires into my body isn't going to turn around and say it's wrong to fulfill them whether in the bonds of marriage or not.

So you think you're going to be hit by a bolt of lightning if you go to bed with me?

It is said that having sex on the Jewish sabbath is a double mitzvah—which means "good deed."

Male: I'm free tonight. Would you like me to come over and help you study?
Female: That's okay, I like to study the Bible in private.

Poetic Lines

No guts, no glory.

All talk, no action.

All show, no go.

The blacker the berry, the sweeter the fruit.

Birds do it and fly, old folks do it and die, so why not you and I?

Let's go spark in the dark.

You can't tease me and leave me.

Musical Lines

Want to play duets in my room?

We could make beautiful music together.

Close your eyes and just sit back and listen to the music.

The stereo in my bedroom is better than the one out here.

He: Do you want to go upstairs and listen to some records?
She: No, thanks. I'm in a rock band and if I hear one more note my ears will fall off.

Chorus Lines

Come on! All college girls do it.

. . . But every other girl I've ever gone out with has said yes.

If you don't try it, you'll be a square.

It's normal.

Him: I don't see any reason why we shouldn't have sex together. Everyone else is doing it.
Her: That's great. Then I guess you won't have any problem finding someone else.

You're the only girl I've gone out with this length of time that hasn't.

Fishing Lines

What'cha doing tonight, baby?

Don't I know you from somewhere?

You feel up to doing something slick?

Isn't it hot in here?

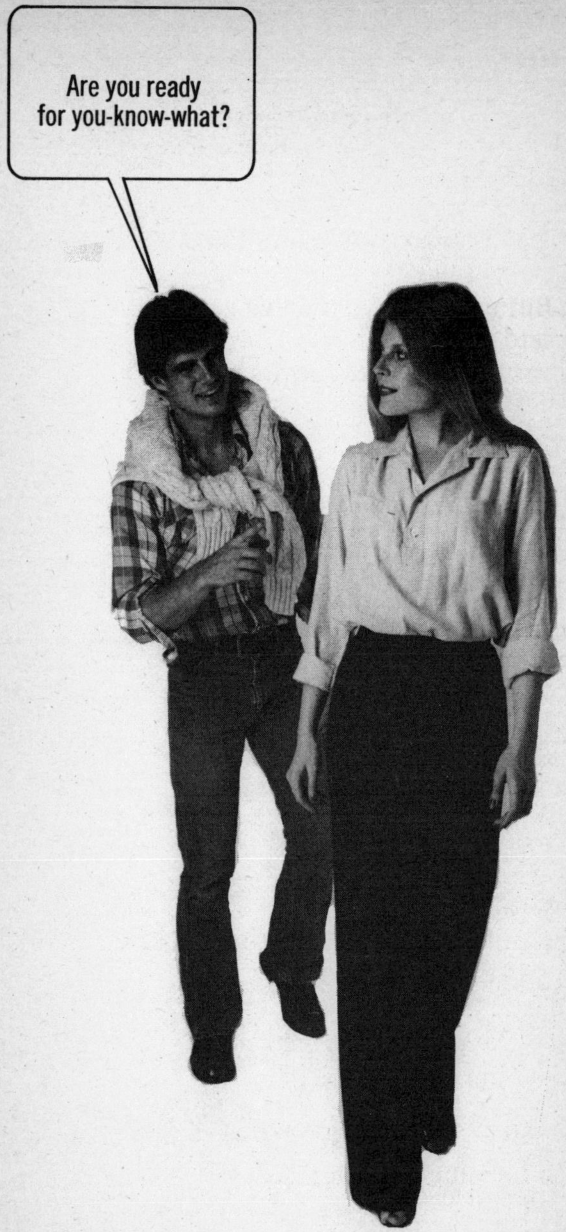
Are you ready
for you-know-what?

Scout Lines

I promise I won't hurt you.

I'll still respect you tomorrow.

I promise you won't get pregnant.

I'm prepared.

Don't worry, I'm clean.

I promise I won't tell.

Honest, I'll pull out in time.

(No) Waiting Lines

Come on! Most girls aren't virgins by the time they get to high school.

Please, I'm going away in three weeks and won't see you again.

If you don't have sex by the time you're sixteen, you'll become a lesbian.

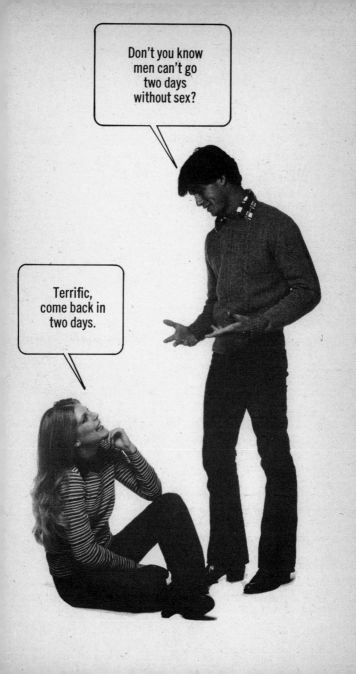

Him: We don't have to waste time sitting here talking.
Her: So don't waste your time; talk to somebody else.

He: I'm going to get a drink, and when I return we'll be together for the night.
She: When you return I'll be gone.

He: I'll be leaving tomorrow . . . Don't you want me to be able to say I had a nice weekend?
She: Sure. But if that's the only way you can have a nice time with me, forget it.

Him: Do you want to go to bed?
Her: No.
Him: Neither do I, so let's hurry up and get it over with.

(Out-and-Out) Lie Lines

You're the first girl I really ever loved—so please go to bed with me.

When we go to bed together, it will be "making love," not "screwing."

You'll never get to know me better any other way.

The hookers usually pay *me* afterwards.

I want to make you feel like a woman.

Why don't you relax? I promise I won't bite.

The One-Sided Line
Advice to the Be-lined

A female student of mine called me on the phone, desperate for an appointment.

She: You must see me. I'm in despair and you're the only one who can help me.
Me: Well, tell me briefly what it's about.
She: My boyfriend insists on my having sex with him. He feels that it's important to test the relationship, and in this modern age only up-tight people wait until marriage.
Me: So, what are your objections?
She: I'm religious—Catholic. I really believe in my religion, and I care about what my parents would think. But he says if I really loved him none of that would matter. But I really love him and it still matters. What should I do? If you say I'm old-fashioned or neurotic about it, I'll go along with it. Please tell me what to do.
Me: I'll tell you exactly what my opinion is, even though what you actually do is none of my business.

She: Yes, yes!

Me: Don't have sex with him.

She: Oh, I'm so relieved. I was afraid you'd say I was uptight or something.

Me: If I were you, I'd say to him: "If you really loved me, you wouldn't put this kind of pressure on me."

She: Hey, that's a good one. It never occurred to me. Thanks. I'll call you to let you know what happens.

Some time later, these conversations took place:

She: Honey, I thought about it and I've decided. If you really loved me, you wouldn't put pressure on me to have sex, knowing that I care about being Catholic and all.

He (after a ten-second pause): You've got a point. I never thought about it that way.

She: I'm glad you see it my way. I'll be back in a minute. I have to make a call.

She: Dr. Gordon, I can't tell you how grateful I am. It worked.

Me: I'm glad.

Read Between the Lines

We can't keep the engine runnin', but we can keep warm.

No, I want to be more than good friends.

How about a beautiful relationship?

<u>Relationship Lines</u>

Sex is fifty percent of every relationship. To really know someone, you have to know them sexually.

Sex is something beautiful between two people.

Our relationship will become stagnant without it.

Sex is the most important thing in a lasting relationship.

You don't have to if you don't want to—it should be a two-way thing. But it would help our relationship grow.

We were made for each other.

That's the way I can show my love for you. It's the only way I can truly express my feelings.

Male: The only thing standing in the way of making our relationship a deep and lasting one is that you won't give your whole self to me. Trust me.
Female: If we can't develop a deep and meaningful relationship without sex, we'll never have one with it.

Is It Really Love?

Love "just is"—so a lot of us think. Yet, as a central cause of concern for millions of people falling in and out of it, one might think we'd have more to say about love than is presented in "soaps," "ads," "rock" and films. One thing we know for sure is love has little or nothing to do with the toothpaste you use, the car you drive or even how G.I.B.* you are.

In the world we live in, love often gets confused with money, sex, or being "turned on" by a part of a person (breasts, ankles, behinds). *Warning:* You can't have a conversation with a behind (even if it's a smart ass) or a fantasy (the person you love doesn't even know you exist).

Perhaps we can't define love itself but we sure can tell if we're in a good or a bad "scene." And it's really not that difficult to figure out if we are in a mature or an immature love affair.

Immature love is exhausting. While you may go around "being in love" you will likely be "too tired" to shower, study or shoulder any responsibilities around the house. After all, you are "in love." You have what is called a hostile-dependent relationship. You can't stand to be with the person you are supposed to love and you can't stand to be without that person. When you are together there are fights and arguments. One of you will often keep repeating "Do you

*Good-In-Bed

love me, do you really love me?" (Say no, and you'll have your first conversation that way.)

A *mature* love affair is energizing. You have time and energy to shower, study and take out the garbage. You don't tell anyone about it (people just know by observing the amount of energy you have). And when you are together you enjoy it (this is not to say that you never argue or disagree). And you discover very quickly that a good relationship (even more so a marriage) is the beginning of a journey— together and apart—to discover all the things in life that you cannot secure from each other.

If I were to list the ten most important aspects in a love relationship (or a marriage) it would look like this:

1. Loving and caring for one another
2. Being able to communicate with each other
3. Having a sense of humor
4. *
5. *
6. *
7. *
8. *
9. Being sexually fulfilled
10. Learning how to clean the house together

Do I really mean to suggest that sex is not important? No—of the some 7,326 things that are important in life, sex is still one of the top ten.

---

*I haven't figured this one out yet—you fill it in for yourself.

It-Can-Be-Better Lines

You'll get just as much out of it as I will.

I'd like to get to know you better.

You haven't experienced full womanhood till you lose your virginity.

I think we're already such good friends, we'd make even more terrific lovers.

(After some necking and petting) You liked it so far, didn't you?

If we have sex, all our problems will work out and we'll get along better.

I've never made love before either, so we can experience something new together.

I really love you. And the closeness we share when I make love to you makes me feel really good inside.

There's no way I can know you better than by having sex with you. It is the highest expression of friendship or love.

Almost-Convincing Lines

Oh, it feels so good! Don't you want to please me?

What's the matter, do you think it will ruin your reputation?

You know that you really want it.

We don't have to be in love to have sex, just friends.

You know, you're really a beautiful person.

I want to turn you on, too. I don't want to get anything off you.

Touching Lines

Just spend the night with me. I just want to hold you all night.

People don't touch anymore. We need to communicate with our bodies. It's beautiful, and I'd love sharing that part of life with you.

Hot-and-Bothered-
Without-the-Payoff Lines

You just can't stop after building me up so. I'll hurt all night.

Why are you here, if you don't want to go all the way?

I'm all worked up. You can't leave me; we'll *have* to now.

You really know how to hurt a guy.

I had to beg my brother to let me use his car tonight—and now you won't cooperate.

Time Lines

Do you want to stay a virgin all your life?

You won't get pregnant the first time.

Let's do it one time for a little while.

I ain't gonna wait forever.

It only hurts for a minute.

Him: Don't leave. I have an alarm clock.
Her: Well, I have an alarm clock too. But it doesn't run fast, so I prefer it over yours.

He: We've been seeing each other for a few weeks; it's about time we got into heavy sex.
She: Is that what time your Mickey Mouse watch says it is?

Male: Do you want to watch the sun rise in the morning?
Female: Just the sun.

Life Lines

Him: Come on, you want it as much as I do. Stop fighting yourself.
Her: If that's true, you must not want it very much.

He: I won't hurt you, and I'll pull out in time.
She: I think I'll pull out of this relationship first!

Male: There's nothing to be afraid of.
Female: It's a good thing you feel that way, because I think I hear my boyfriend, the football player, coming up the stairs.

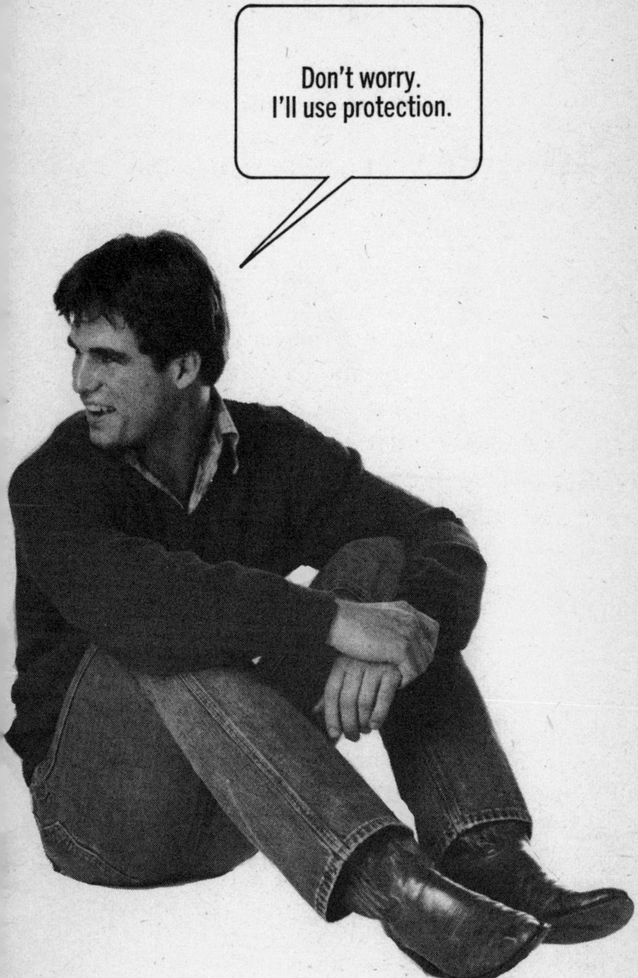
Don't worry.
I'll use protection.

High Lines

The more I drink the better you look.

This is terrible; I shouldn't drink like this. I get horny when I drink.

Want to come to my room and get high?

You make me so nervous every time you reject me that you're driving me to drink.

Here, have another drink. I won't take advantage of you.

Low Lines

What's wrong with you? Don't you like men?

Are you a dyke or something?

You're my wife and you owe it to me.

I've known you long enough. So if you don't do it tonight, we can just forget it.

Don't you want to prove you love me?

You shouldn't waste such a beautiful body on just one man. You should share it. Don't tell me you're selfish?

Light Lines

Male: Aren't these bright lights bothering you?
Female: Not me. Would you like to borrow my sunglasses?

Him: I can really turn you on.
Her: The only thing that needs to be turned on in here is the lights.

Heavy Lines

I have such a heavy load! If you don't, I'll hurt.

Hard Lines

THE ULTIMATE HARD (-ON) LINE: When a man starts, he can't stop.

Male: I could have scored with that girl, but I'd rather be with you.
Female: If you're so eager to score, I'll go find that girl. Because you won't score with me.

Soft and Romantic Lines

I need you.

This will make our love complete.

I've really missed you.

You're not just another face or number in the crowd. I really love you.

This will just draw us closer together.

I love you, and this is the best way to express my feelings.

I've never had any experience with this either, so it will be a beautiful learning experience for us both.

We're getting married someday anyway, aren't we?

I'll take care of everything.

Outside Lines
Excerpts from Hundreds of Unsolicited Letters

One of the most popular lines in the Navy is, "If I wanted to go to bed with someone, I would have rented a whore." Crude, yes, but it gives a distinct impression that the woman is respected for herself, not her body. Almost instantly, the woman can relax, not worry about how she's going to fend this young man off, and start having a good time. Close feelings develop, of course, and now the woman feels she can be seduced with respect.

I was a college senior for a semester program. (Herein let me insert that I'm white.) My date was a young, modishly dressed black man. He tried all the various approaches. I kept saying no and that I was getting tired of hearing it. Finally, in desperation, he said, "Look, you're young, white, from a totally middle-class background in the midwest. I'm older, black, from a ghetto area and have worked my way up. Think of it as a cultural exchange." My reply: "Is that sort of like Hands Across the Sea?"

My date had, with persistence and logic, gotten me to agree that "it would be fun," "it would hurt no one," "it could do no harm" and several other such statements. Having no more logic left, but having no desire either, for more than a date, I was forced to hit below the belt. "Why not?" he asked, finally. "Because you don't appeal to me," I answered.

I'll put it in just a little and take it right out.
—Someone Who Learned Better the Hard Way.

I know a boy who stands near the main exit of Central High School here, waiting for the rest of the students to come pouring out. He has a very simple line that's right to the point. When he sees a gal who appeals to him, he asks, "Do you want to screw?" He gets his face slapped a lot, but he also gets a lot of screwing.

The line most frequently used by young men, when I was young, was how painful it was to get aroused without "satisfaction." After marriage, the line is how much more interesting, better dressed, understanding, warm or loving the other woman is than his wife.

I was sixteen and my steady boyfriend used psychological pressure. He pressured me constantly by telling me such things as: "You're the only girl I've ever wanted to sleep with," and "I can't stand to be near you if I can't have you." He also told me he was a virgin and had never had sex. Also, "If I can't have you, I have no reason to live."

Male to Female: "I promise we won't actually do it. Just make me feel good." "As long as we don't actually do it, there'll be no harm done." Then . . . "You can't leave me like this!"

Male (at age sixteen and engaged): I love you as much as I will when we are married—and we both want to.
Female (now twenty-five, deserted and sorry): Let's get in the back seat!

Male (at age sixteen): I want you to be my first one!
Female (at age twenty-four, who has no idea where he is now): What good is that to me?

A line is dependent on the circumstances. It depends on who you're with and where. Lines are tailored for special incidents: "Haven't I seen you before?" "I'd really like to get to know you better." "Let's go out for a beer." "I dreamed about you last night." "You have beautiful— (eyes, hair, skin, features)." Flatter them.

—Male, age twenty-one

Inside Lines

Upstairs and Downstairs

Wanna go upstairs and watch TV?

Would you like to come to my room and see my peacock feather?

You're a very attractive girl and I'd like to get to know your mind, so why don't you come over to my room tonight and we'll be just the two of us, etcetera, etcetera?

I just decorated my room. Why don't you come up and take a look at it?

Have you ever seen the inside of a fraternity house?

You should see the poster in my room.

He: How would you like to go upstairs and make it?
She: But the kitchen is over here.

At the guy's apartment: You're the only girl I've ever had here. You'd be the only one to ever do it in my bed.

Lines To Cry By

I'm so frustrated, there must be something wrong with me. Maybe you can help me overcome my difficulty.

How can you do this to me?

Why not? What's the matter, is it me?

But if you don't go to bed with me, it'll force me to homosexuality.

Why don't you trust me? I'm a good Jewish boy.

Oh, I've got so much love and no one to give it to!

C'mon, do me a favor—turn me on.

You don't love me.

I'm afraid I'm gay. Help me prove to myself that I'm not.

I have a hard time getting an erection. You look sensational, I bet you could get me there.

I've never had sex before; you'll be the first. Doesn't that make you feel good?

It's selfish of a woman not to want to share herself completely with a man she cares about. I'm willing to share myself and the responsibilities of sex with you.

After heavy petting session: It's been so long since I did it, I've probably forgotten how.

Plain Lines

And Responses Women Would Like to Have Given, Now That They Are Older and Wiser

Him: I feel that because you're a virgin you should have your first experience by me, because I'm considered great.
Her: No, thank you. I do just fine by myself.

He: It's getting crowded in here, let's go somewhere quiet and talk.
She: No, thank you. I enjoy being in crowds.

Male: Why don't you come over here where it's more comfortable?
Female: No thanks, it's comfortable being this far away from you.

He: I love you and I believe it is right, but the final decision is up to you.
She: I am also sure about loving you but I'm not emotionally ready, so my decision is "no."

Him: Let's go to the bedroom where we can be alone.
Her: No thanks. I'm sure what you have in mind for us in the bedroom isn't what I had in mind for the evening.

Male: But you know how much I like you.
Female: I know how much you like me and I like me, too. So no!

He: Why don't we go up to my room and talk for a while? There's more privacy there.
She: No, thanks. When it comes to talking I'm really versatile, I can talk anywhere. Right here is fine.

Whine Lines

Just this once!

Don't drive me crazy!

Pleeeease! ! !

Female Lines

Do you have the notes on the bio lecture on muscles?

Don't be afraid. You can touch any part of my body.

You're all I've got. My father traveled and I never had someone I could count on.

Do you want to come home with me tonight?

Would you like me to seduce you?

I'm great at giving back massages, but only if you take off your shirt. How about it?

I'm getting my friend tomorrow anyway.

I took one of my mother's pills.

Want to see my scar?

Are you ticklish?

A la Mae West: Is that a pistol in your pocket or are you really glad to see me?

Let me get your rocks off.

Where have you been hiding?

If Lines

If you don't have sex, then you can never reach the ultimate in a relationship.

If you really love me, then you'll go to bed with me.

If you don't, then I'm going to break up with you.

If you love me, then prove it.

If you love me, then you'll let me because I ain't had none in a long time.

Male: If you don't stay over, then you'll never know what you're missing.
Female: Yes, I do. That's why the answer is *no!*

He: If you really loved me, then you would . . .
She: If you really love me, then we can wait for our relationship to grow even more.

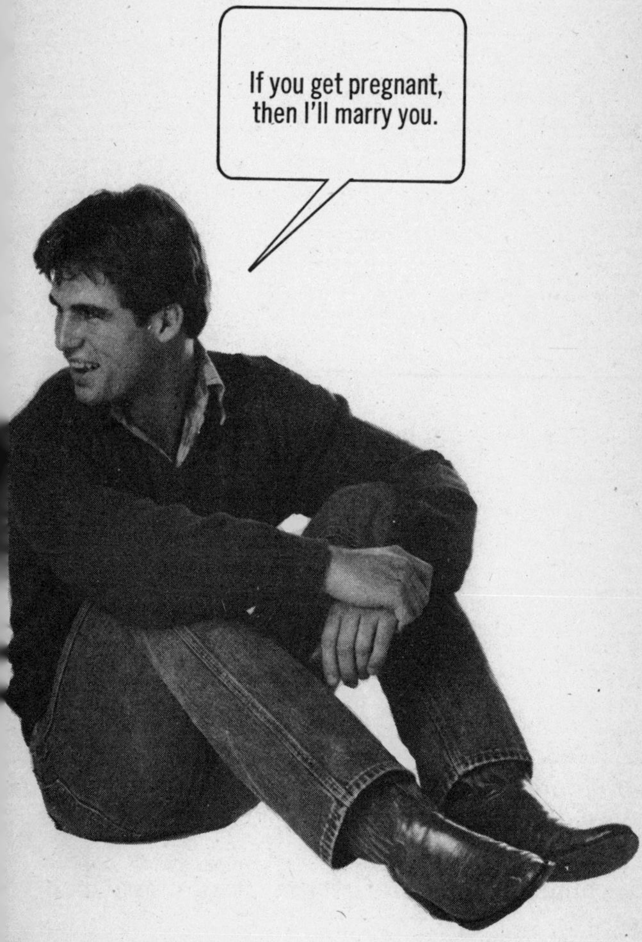
If you get pregnant, then I'll marry you.

But-Honey Lines

But honey, if I love you and you love me, then it's a natural thing.

But honey, we'll do it for a second; just for *one* second.

But honey, you are a part of me and I am a part of you, so let's become one.

But honey, nobody will know but us two.

But honey, I love you.

But honey, why not let me make you feel good?

But honey, everyone is doing it.

Aw-Come-On Lines

Aw, come on! Try it only one fast one. It will be over before you know it. Just close your eyes and open your legs.

Aw, come on! After the first time it's going to feel good.

Aw, come on! I want you to have my baby.

Aw, come on! I want you to be all mine.

Aw, come on! It will make us closer.

Aw, come on! For old time's sake.

Aw, come on, baby! I've got a hard-on that won't quit.

Aw, come on! You're here now, just relax.

Aw, come on! You know you want to, so what's stopping you?

Aw, come on! Please don't leave me like this.

Don't Worry Lines

Don't worry, I'll be gentle.

Don't worry, it's the most natural thing on earth.

Don't worry, I will still respect you in the morning.

Don't worry, you won't get pregnant.

Don't worry, it doesn't hurt.

Don't worry, when I'm ready to come, I'll pull out.

Don't worry, I can't have children.

Don't worry, if anything happens I'll marry you and take care of you.

Don't worry, you'll only bleed a little.

Once-In-A-Lifetime Lines

You only live once.

Awww! Come on! Just this once. You can't knock it till you've tried it.

I'll still respect you tomorrow.

Let's do it so I'll have something to remember you by after you're gone.

Pregnant Lines*

Nothing will happen.

It's late, why don't you stay overnight? I promise I won't touch you.

What else did I go on a blind date for?

You'll enjoy it.

Let's get to know you better.

If you really love me . . .

If I only knew you were that type of girl.

What's wrong with two lonely people trying to make each other happy?

You can't put water back up over the dam.

You know I love you.

*"Successful" lines volunteered by out-of-wedlock—and abandoned—pregnant teenagers.

Why can't we have sex? Nobody will know it but us.

Anything you want, I will get it for you.

I know when to get up.

I'll use some protection.

I'm yours and you're mine, so let's make love.

Let's go into the bedroom.

I promise I won't make a mistake.

Go put on your nightgown.

Turn the TV off.

When's your mother coming home?

I *can't* get you pregnant; I can't have kids.

You're on the pill!

You can't get pregnant; it's not that time of month.

Lines To Nibble On

Why don't you come over and eat breakfast at my place?

I would like to stay for dinner . . . and breakfast.

How would you like to lay down and digest your dinner with me?

Male: Hey, if you sleep over here tonight, I'll make you a really fantastic breakfast tomorrow morning.
Female: If you're so interested in flaunting your culinary talents, why didn't you say so in the first place?

Late-and-Out-of-Gas Lines

It doesn't make any sense for me to go home now, since it's already four a.m. and we're going to play tennis at eight.

I'm too tired to take you back home.

I don't think my car has enough gas to get you home.

It's really pretty late to go back. How about staying over and I'll take you back in the morning.

I've got no place to stay tonight; mind if I stay with you?

Lines To Make You Drowsy

I'm tired, let's lay down.

Do you want to spend the night?

Hey, I'm pretty tired. Are you tired?

The Ultimate Lines

He: If you really love me, you'll have sex with me.
She: If you really love me, you won't lay your trip on me.

Male: You have one big, middle-class hangup.
Female: It's you who has the hang-up—one big hard-on.

Him: You can always get an abortion.
Her: ???

Lines To Say "No" By

No.

Keep your paws off me.

I'm not in love with you.

I'm not in the mood.

It's a special thing to me.

You're not my type.

I have hay fever really bad.

I have a headache.

I'm tired.

The baby is crying.

Cut it out!

Why should I?

Lay off!

I don't know you well enough.

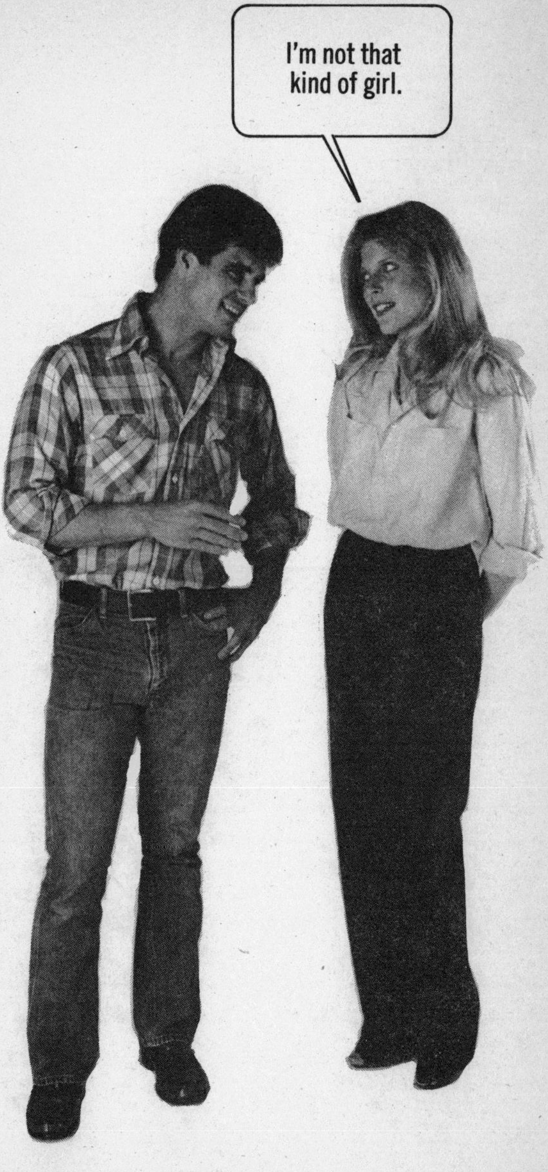
I'm not that
kind of girl.

No; it's against my religion. (Boy, do they soak that one up.)

I don't want to lose my virginity.

I really don't feel like it.

I feel if we wait you will believe I'm more interested in you than a one night stand.

A Foolish-Adult Line

Kids know everything about sex these days.*

*Letter from a fourteen-year-old girl in Nebraska (received by the author in 1977):

> Dear Mr. Sol Gordon,
>
> I come from a family where I have learned sex from my friends. My mother don't mention it to me. And I still don't know what most of sex and love is all about. So I would like to know because I'm only 14 years of age. And I've seen my friends get pregnant. I'd like to know what it's all about. Thank you.

Postscript

What's my line? "No one can make you feel inferior without your consent."

Note to Reader

A second collection of lines is already in the works. Would you help? Would you send me your lines, or lines used on you? Please specify your age and the circumstances. If you wish acknowledgment, include your name and address. Otherwise, all lines will be kept confidential; if used, your name will not be given.

We are especially interested in lines in current use, in lines used years ago and in ethnic lines.

We would be grateful if teachers collected lines from their students and discussed their implications in class.

We are also collecting superstitions about sexuality. Which ones did you grow up on?

ABOUT THE AUTHOR

As one of the leading American sex educators and psychologists, SOL GORDON is renowned for his insight, humor and honest approach to young people. "People say sex education leads to promiscuity," says Dr. Gordon. "But last year *without* proper education, there were one million pregnant teenage girls—one million!" Gordon's solution is more and better communication. And his new book, *You Would If You Loved Me*, is yet another creative attempt to open the channels. Dr. Gordon teaches child and family studies, and is the director of the prominent Institute for Family Research and Education in Syracuse. He is the author of *You: A Survival Guide for Youth, The Sexual Adolescent* and *Parenting: A Guide for Young People*. His books, television appearances and lectures have earned him the trust and respect of teenagers, parents, grandparents and fellow educators everywhere.

TEENAGERS FACE LIFE AND LOVE

Choose books filled with fun and adventure, discovery and disenchantment, failure and conquest, triumph and tragedy, life and love.

☐	13359	**THE LATE GREAT ME** Sandra Scoppettone	$1.95
☐	13691	**HOME BEFORE DARK** Sue Ellen Bridgers	$1.75
☐	12501	**PARDON ME, YOU'RE STEPPING ON MY EYEBALL!** Paul Zindel	$1.95
☐	11091	**A HOUSE FOR JONNIE O.** Blossom Elfman	$1.95
☐	12025	**ONE FAT SUMMER** Robert Lipsyte	$1.75
☐	13184	**I KNOW WHY THE CAGED BIRD SINGS** Maya Angelou	$2.25
☐	13013	**ROLL OF THUNDER, HEAR MY CRY** Mildred Taylor	$1.95
☐	12741	**MY DARLING, MY HAMBURGER** Paul Zindel	$1.95
☐	12420	**THE BELL JAR** Sylvia Plath	$2.50
☐	13897	**WHERE THE RED FERN GROWS** Wilson Rawls	$2.25
☐	11829	**CONFESSIONS OF A TEENAGE BABOON** Paul Zindel	$1.95
☐	11838	**OUT OF LOVE** Hilma Wolitzer	$1.50
☐	13352	**SOMETHING FOR JOEY** Richard E. Peck	$1.95
☐	13440	**SUMMER OF MY GERMAN SOLDIER** Bette Greene	$1.95
☐	13693	**WINNING** Robin Brancato	$1.95
☐	13628	**IT'S NOT THE END OF THE WORLD** Judy Blume	$1.95

Buy them at your local bookstore or use this handy coupon for ordering:

Bantam Book Catalog

Here's your up-to-the-minute listing of over 1,400 titles by your favorite authors.

This illustrated, large format catalog gives a description of each title. For your convenience, it is divided into categories in fiction and non-fiction—gothics, science fiction, westerns, mysteries, cookbooks, mysticism and occult, biographies, history, family living, health, psychology, art.

So don't delay—take advantage of this special opportunity to increase your reading pleasure.

Just send us your name and address and 50¢ (to help defray postage and handling costs).